There is in every person an
inward sea,
and in that sea there is an
island
and on that island there is an
altar
and standing guard before
that alter
is the "angel with the flaming
sword."
Nothing can get by that angel
to be placed upon that altar
unless it has the mark of your
inner authority.
Nothing passes
"the angel with the flaming
sword"
to be placed upon your altar
unless it be part of
"the fluid area of your
consent."
This is your crucial link with the
Eternal.[1]

(Howard Thurman)

Contemporary Fiction by Susan McGeown:

Recipe for Disaster
Rules for Survival
A Well Behaved Woman's Life
The Butler Did It
Joining The Club
Embracing The Truth
The Best Secret (Coming)

Historical Fiction by Susan McGeown:

A Garden Walled Around Trilogy:
Call Me Bear
Call Me Elle
Call Me Survivor
Rosamund's Bower
No Darkness So Great
Windermere Plantation

Nonfiction by Susan McGeown:

Biblical Women and Who They Hooked Up With
Biblical Warrior Women and Their Weapons
Jerusalem Times:
JT: The Jesus of Nazareth Edition
JT: The Twelve Apostles Edition
God's Phoenix Woman
The Rise of the Mighty (A Study of Acts)
What We Believe (A Study of Romans)
C.S. Lewis & Me
Old Testament 101
The Parables of Jesus
A Book of Thanks
Prayer & Me
A Book of Blessing
Prayer & Me
A Book of Blessings
A Verse A Day
Words Worth Remembering
Advice on Marriage and Friendship From Someone Who's Been There
A Book of Prayers Worth Repeating

Prayers Worth Repeating

Talking With Our Lord

By Susan McGeown

Faith Inspired Books

Published by Faith Inspired Books
3 Kathleen Place, Bridgewater, New Jersey 08807
susanmcgeown@faithinspiredbooks.com
www.FaithInspiredBooks.com

ISBN: 978-1-946268-09-9

The quoted ideas expressed in this book (but not the scripture verses) are not, in all cases, exact quotations but rather obtained from secondary sources, primarily print media. In every case, the author has made every effort to maintain the speaker's original intent. While every effort was made to ensure the accuracy of these sources, the accuracy cannot be guaranteed. For additions, deletions, corrections, or clarifications please contact Susan McGeown at the above address.

Bibliographic credit appears at the end of this work.

Christmas, 2023

Dearest Eternal Friends,

Once again, we are at the end of the year and finally I have had the time to put together another "Gift Book" of sorts. In the midst of our COVID pandemic, there was no giftbooks because there was no in-person meeting and I couldn't figure out how I could deliver them all. Thanks be to God we are able to fellowship together in person once again. (YAY!)

This book is inspired from much of my seminary reading and research; I actually had begun to write down, for my own personal use, certain prayers that particularly spoke to me and then I thought, "Hey, wait a minute…I could do more with this…" I pray that you will be blessed by these words of those who have gone before us. Seminary has taught me that we stand on the shoulders of these brothers and sisters and, just as importantly, we are destined to become the critical "next layer" to support those who come after us. Let us have confident hope (Romans 15:13) that we will, indeed, be those that bless others with our shining, vibrant faith in Jesus Christ!

This is my simple prayer which I try to start each day with:

"Lord, show me what You are doing today,
and how I can be a part of it.

Love and Blessings,

Sue

XXOO

TABLE OF CONTENTS

PRAYERS FROM OTHER CHRISTIANS 33

ABOUT PRAYER

Let me first talk with you about what prayer is not. It is not a special incantation to get God to change or grant a wish. In fact, prayer is not in any way a mechanism to get what you want – regardless of your perceived importance or need. Whether one person or a thousand pray for something, prayer will not change God's mind about the course of action God believes to be best. You see, God has consistently – without exception – always worked in tangent with humanity; we were designed to be God's partner in all earthly endeavors. In fact, we are described biblically as God's hands and feet! (Romans 10:15) It is humanity – God's believers empowered with the Spirit – that are to be the key force that causes change in the world. (Matthew 5:13-16) It is through prayer, that the Spirit transforms us and helps us do what is best; prayer is The Transformational Avenue to becoming our best selves.

Prayer for a believer is like breathing is to a living being; it just cannot be separated. Yet, if you are like me, you sometimes struggle with prayer. There's the concern that you may not be doing it "correctly;" there's the terrifying possibility that you may someday be asked to do it out loud in front of others, there's the intimidating moments when you listen to others pray and you know you will never, ever be able to pray so eloquently; there are the frustrating times when you prayed desperately and consistently for something that was of the utmost need … and your prayers "didn't work," there are those awful times when things are so complicated that you simply don't know what to pray for, and there are the worst times when you feel so low, so lost, so alone that prayer becomes almost like your last desperate attempt to …survive.

The interesting thing about all these above concerns is that I'm fairly certain that all human beings on the planet have had these thoughts at least at some points in their life. Don't you agree? For me, that means that these concerns are to be dismissed; if God wants us to pray God must be willing to take our prayers … imperfect and halting and inexperienced though they may be. We must remember that humanity was created for a relationship with God rooted in love. Think about those you love and are closest to; what do you desire most with them? Isn't a relationship rooted in love – no matter how halting, imperfect, and inexperienced it may be – the most important thing we hope for? Now, translate that to God and you.

Below are just a few of my favorite quotes; in my own words. (That alone could be another book really.) Searching "prayer quotes" on the Internet will keep you very busy. Following these few brief quotes, I could not resist giving some Scripture verses in response to the above listed concerns we often have regarding prayer. You see, God thinks of everything; God has already been before us preparing the way.

Favorite Prayer Quotes (My version, but not my quote):

- Why should we pray? Because Jesus did.
- Prayer is the act of seeing reality from God's point of view.
- We don't change things when we pray; prayer changes us.

- Prayer doesn't prepare us for the big work; prayer is the big work.
- God will either give us what we ask for or give us what we would have asked for if we knew everything.
- Prayer: Just. Do. It.

Scripture to counteract your prayer concerns:

There's the concern that you may not be doing it "correctly".

Philippians 4:6 Do not be anxious about anything, but in everything by prayer and supplication with thanksgiving let your requests be made known to God.

There's the terrifying possibility that you may someday be asked to do it out loud in front of others.

Jeremiah 33:3 Call to me, and I will answer you and will tell you great and hidden things that you have not known.

There's the intimidating moments when you listen to others pray and you know you will never, ever be able to pray so eloquently.

I Corinthians 14:15 What should I do then? I will pray with the spirit, but I will pray with the mind also; I will sing praise with the spirit, but I will sing praise with the mind also.

There are the frustrating times when you prayed desperately and consistently for something that was of the utmost need … and your prayers "didn't work".

I John 5:14-15 And this is the boldness we have in him, that if we ask anything according to his will, he hears us. 15 And if we know that he hears us in whatever we ask, we know that we have obtained the requests made of him.

There are those awful times when things are so complicated that you simply don't know what to pray for.

Romans 8:28 Likewise the Spirit helps us in our weakness, for we do not know how to pray as we ought, but that very Spirit intercedes with groanings too deep for words.

There are the worst times when you feel so low, so lost, so alone that prayer becomes almost like your last desperate attempt to ...survive.

Exodus 14:14 The LORD will fight for you, and you have only to keep still.

PRAYERS FROM SCRIPTURE

2

DAVID'S PRAYER OF PRAISE

I & II Samuel, I & II Kings, I & II Chronicles, Psalms

Facts About David:

✓ In I Samuel 13:14, he is described as a "man after God's own heart."

✓ David was Ruth (and Boaz's) great grandson. (See the book of Ruth!) (I Chronicles 2:12)

✓ From Bethlehem, David was the youngest of many sons. (I Samuel 16:10-11)

✓ He was a shepherd and a musician and was chosen by God to be "the anointed one." (I Samuel 10:1, 16:14, 17:34-37)

✓ He screwed up a lot (adultery, murder…) but always crawled back to God with genuine, heartfelt forgiveness.

✓ Despite all his mistakes, his heart was for God and the Messiah, Jesus.

Psalm 63[3]

1 O God, you are my God;
I earnestly search for you.
My soul thirsts for you;
my whole body longs for you
in this parched and weary land
where there is no water.
2 I have seen you in your sanctuary
and gazed upon your power and glory.
3 Your unfailing love is better than life itself;
how I praise you!

[4] I will praise you as long as I live,
lifting up my hands to you in prayer.
[5] You satisfy me more than the richest feast.
I will praise you with songs of joy.
[6] I lie awake thinking of you,
meditating on you through the night.
[7] Because you are my helper,
I sing for joy in the shadow of your wings.
[8] I cling to you;
your strong right hand holds me securely.

DAVID'S PRAYER FOR LIFE

Psalm 139

[1] O LORD, you have examined my heart
and know everything about me.
[2] You know when I sit down or stand up.
You know my thoughts even when I'm far away.
[3] You see me when I travel
and when I rest at home.
You know everything I do.
[4] You know what I am going to say
even before I say it, LORD.
[5] You go before me and follow me.
You place your hand of blessing on my head.
[6] Such knowledge is too wonderful for me,
too great for me to understand!

[7] I can never escape from your Spirit!
I can never get away from your presence!
[8] If I go up to heaven, you are there;
if I go down to the grave,[a] you are there.
[9] If I ride the wings of the morning,
if I dwell by the farthest oceans,

[10] even there your hand will guide me,
and your strength will support me.
[11] I could ask the darkness to hide me
and the light around me to become night—
12 but even in darkness I cannot hide from you.
To you the night shines as bright as day.
Darkness and light are the same to you.

[13] You made all the delicate, inner parts of my body
and knit me together in my mother's womb.
[14] Thank you for making me so wonderfully complex!
Your workmanship is marvelous—how well I know it.
[15] You watched me as I was being formed in utter seclusion,
as I was woven together in the dark of the womb.
[16] You saw me before I was born.
Every day of my life was recorded in your book.
Every moment was laid out
before a single day had passed.

[17] How precious are your thoughts about me,[b] O God.
They cannot be numbered!
[18] I can't even count them;
they outnumber the grains of sand!
And when I wake up,
you are still with me!

[19] O God, if only you would destroy the wicked!
Get out of my life, you murderers!
[20] They blaspheme you;
your enemies misuse your name.
[21] O LORD, shouldn't I hate those who hate you?
Shouldn't I despise those who oppose you?
[22] Yes, I hate them with total hatred,
for your enemies are my enemies.

[23] Search me, O God, and know my heart;
test me and know my anxious thoughts.

[24] Point out anything in me that offends you,
and lead me along the path of everlasting life.

DAVID'S PRAYER OF CONFIDENCE & TRUST

Psalm 23

This is from the Common English Bible[4] Translation

The LORD is my shepherd.
I lack nothing.
[2] He lets me rest in grassy meadows;
he leads me to restful waters;
[3] he keeps me [a] alive.
He guides me in proper paths
for the sake of his good name.

[4] Even when I walk through the darkest valley,
I fear no danger because you are with me.
Your rod and your staff—
they protect me.

[5] You set a table for me
right in front of my enemies.
You bathe my head in oil;
my cup is so full it spills over!
[6] Yes, goodness and faithful love
will pursue me all the days of my life,
and I will live in the LORD's house
as long as I live.

MOSES' PRAYER OF BLESSING

Exodus

Facts About Moses:

✓ He was born into slavery at a time when all Jewish boy babies were to be immediately killed.

✓ He was raised by an Egyptian princess and had all the privileges of an Egyptian prince.

✓ He was a very reluctant leader who many believed had a stuttering problem.

✓ He wasn't called to be the one to lead the Israelite nation to freedom until he was eighty!

Numbers 6:24-26

24 'May the LORD bless you
and protect you.
25 May the LORD smile on you
and be gracious to you.
26 May the LORD show you his favor
and give you his peace.'

PAUL'S PRAYER FOR EMPOWERMENT

Christian Testament: Acts and numerous additional books

Facts About Paul:

- ✓ He was a highly educated and religious Jew who had the esteemed rank of Pharisee at one point in his life.
- ✓ He originally sought to eradicate Jewish believers who followed "The Way;" the belief that Jesus Christ was the Promised Messiah of the Hebrew Scriptures.
- ✓ He was present at the stoning of the disciple Stephen (he guarded the coats) and was given permission by the Jewish religious authorities to arrest and imprison all those who proclaimed Jesus Christ as Lord.
- ✓ He called himself an apostle[1] and his primary goal and mission was to bring the Mission and Message of Jesus Christ to the Gentiles (non-Jews).
- ✓ He was a prolific writer, responsible for substantial portions of the Christian Scriptures.

Ephesians 3:14-20

14 When I think of all this, I fall to my knees and pray to the Father, 15 the Creator of everything in heaven and on earth.

16 I pray that from his glorious, unlimited resources he will empower you with inner strength through his Spirit.

[1] All those who were considered "apostles" were specifically called by Jesus. Paul, who became an apostle *after* Jesus Christ's crucifixion and resurrection, was called in a vision. Galatians 1:11-17

[17] Then Christ will make his home in your hearts as you
trust in him. Your roots will grow down into God's love
and keep you strong.

[18] And may you have the power to understand, as all
God's people should, how wide, how long, how high,
and how deep his love is.

[19] May you experience the love of Christ, though it is
too great to understand fully.

Then you will be made complete with all the fullness
of life and power that comes from God.

[20] Now all glory to God, who is able, through his
mighty power at work within us, to accomplish
infinitely more than we might ask or think.

MARY'S PRAYER OF JOY

Matthew 1-2, Luke 1-2, select portions of Gospels

<u>Facts About Mary:</u>

- ✓ We know nothing about her early life except that she was young, poor, only marginally formally educated (as all women were at the time) and yet is proclaimed as "favored one" by God via the Angel Gabriel. (Luke 1:28)
- ✓ Her betrothed, Joseph, has no recorded spoken words only obedient actions. He will be directly communicated by God three times.
- ✓ She will be present at the crucifixion as well as at the very beginning of the Apostle's ministry after Jesus Christ's ascension. (Acts 1:14)
- ✓ She bears the Greek description of "Theotokos" which means "Mother of God."
- ✓ Reading her prayer carefully, it is very radical and empowering.

Luke 1:47-55

This is from the Common English Bible[5] Translation

In the depths of who I am I rejoice in God my savior.

48 He has looked with favor on the low status of his servant.

Look! From now on, everyone will consider me highly favored

49 because the mighty one has done great
things for me.
Holy is his name.
50 He shows mercy to everyone,
from one generation to the next,
who honors him as God.
51 He has shown strength with his arm.
He has scattered those with arrogant thoughts and
proud inclinations.
52 He has pulled the powerful down from their
thrones
and lifted up the lowly.
53 He has filled the hungry with good things
and sent the rich away empty-handed.
54 He has come to the aid of his servant Israel,
remembering his mercy,
55 just as he promised to our ancestors,
to Abraham and to Abraham's descendants
forever."

JEREMIAH'S PRAYER OF ENCOURAGEMENT

The Book of Jeremiah & Lamentations

Facts About Jeremiah:

- ✓ He will be the prophet that foretells and then oversees the destruction of Judah and Jerusalem by Babylon.
- ✓ He is often referred to by scholars as the "Weeping Prophet." (That's how bad things were.)
- ✓ He also wrote the book of Lamentations (which is Hebrew for "a passionate expression of grief or sorrow").
- ✓ Despite decades of ministry and (almost never quitting) he will see no visible success.

Jeremiah 17:7-8

7 "But blessed are those who trust in the LORD
and have made the LORD their hope and confidence.
8 They are like trees planted along a riverbank,
with roots that reach deep into the water.
Such trees are not bothered by the heat
or worried by long months of drought.
Their leaves stay green,
and they never stop producing fruit.

JESUS' PRAYER OF INSTRUCTION

The Gospels2 of Matthew, Mark, Luke, & John

Facts About Jesus:

- ✓ There is no world religion that denies the existence of Jesus Christ's earthly existence.
- ✓ Jesus was born into poverty, into a family that was poor in every sense of the word, a minority under an oppressive enemy regime, to a lower class of Jews (Galilean), in a part of the world that was considered "backward" or "insignificant."
- ✓ His message was radically revolutionary in just about every aspect of the practiced Jewish religion at the time of his life.
- ✓ Within his own people and his own religion, he consistently defied those in authority, disobeyed the exclusionary taboos the religious authorities insisted be observed, and ignored all cultural "rules" of proper society.
- ✓ He showed love and acceptance to the despised, rejected, oppressed, forbidden, infamous, and excluded preferring their companionship to those society honored and respected.
- ✓ From earthly perspectives, he had no formal religious training, no official religious authority, and his personal claims about himself justified him as only one of three possibilities: God on earth, a lunatic, or a devil.

---

[2] "Gospels" means "Good News/Story" in Latin/Greek.

- ✓ His Mission and Message (believed or disbelieved) would transform the entire world.

Matthew 6:9-13

(This is the Message[6] Translation)

7-13 "The world is full of so-called prayer warriors who are prayer-ignorant. They're full of formulas and programs and advice, peddling techniques for getting what you want from God. Don't fall for that nonsense. This is your Father you are dealing with, and he knows better than you what you need. With a God like this loving you, you can pray very simply. Like this:

Our Father in heaven,
Reveal who you are.
Set the world right;
Do what's best—
as above, so below.
Keep us alive with three square meals.
Keep us forgiven with you and forgiving others.
Keep us safe from ourselves and the Devil.
You're in charge!
You can do anything you want!
You're ablaze in beauty!
Yes. Yes. Yes.

JESUS' PRAYER FOR YOU PERSONALLY

- ✓ Below is his final prayer, prayed moments before his arrest which would lead to his crucifixion.

John 17

Father, it's time.
Display the bright splendor of your Son
So the Son in turn may show your bright splendor.
You put him in charge of everything human
So he might give real and eternal life to all in his charge.
And this is the real and eternal life:
That they know you,
The one and only true God,
And Jesus Christ, whom you sent.
I glorified you on earth
By completing down to the last detail
What you assigned me to do.
And now, Father, glorify me with your very own splendor,
The very splendor I had in your presence
Before there was a world.

6-12 I spelled out your character in detail
To the men and women you gave me.
They were yours in the first place;
Then you gave them to me,
And they have now done what you said.
They know now, beyond the shadow of a doubt,
That everything you gave me is firsthand from you,
For the message you gave me, I gave them;
And they took it, and were convinced
That I came from you.

They believed that you sent me.
I pray for them.
I'm not praying for the God-rejecting world
But for those you gave me,
For they are yours by right.
Everything mine is yours, and yours mine,
And my life is on display in them.
For I'm no longer going to be visible in the world;
They'll continue in the world
While I return to you.
Holy Father, guard them as they pursue this life
That you conferred as a gift through me,
So they can be one heart and mind
As we are one heart and mind.
As long as I was with them, I guarded them
In the pursuit of the life you gave through me;
I even posted a night watch.
And not one of them got away,
Except for the rebel bent on destruction
(the exception that proved the rule of Scripture).

13-19 Now I'm returning to you.
I'm saying these things in the world's hearing
So my people can experience
My joy completed in them.
I gave them your word;
The godless world hated them because of it,
Because they didn't join the world's ways,
Just as I didn't join the world's ways.
I'm not asking that you take them out of the world
But that you guard them from the Evil One.
They are no more defined by the world
Than I am defined by the world.
Make them holy—consecrated—with the truth;
Your word is consecrating truth.
In the same way that you gave me a mission in the world,

I give them a mission in the world.
I'm consecrating myself for their sakes
So they'll be truth-consecrated in their mission.

20-23 I'm praying not only for them
But also for those who will believe in me
Because of them and their witness about me.
The goal is for all of them to become one heart and mind—
Just as you, Father, are in me and I in you,
So they might be one heart and mind with us.
Then the world might believe that you, in fact, sent me.
The same glory you gave me, I gave them,
So they'll be as unified and together as we are—
I in them and you in me.
Then they'll be mature in this oneness,
And give the godless world evidence
That you've sent me and loved them
In the same way you've loved me.

24-26 Father, I want those you gave me
To be with me, right where I am,
So they can see my glory, the splendor you gave me,
Having loved me
Long before there ever was a world.
Righteous Father, the world has never known you,
But I have known you, and these disciples know
That you sent me on this mission.
I have made your very being known to them—
Who you are and what you do—
And continue to make it known,
So that your love for me
Might be in them
Exactly as I am in them.

JONAH'S PRAYER FROM ROCK BOTTOM

The Book of Jonah

Facts About Jonah:

- ✓ When God initially called him to be a prophet, he promptly got in a boat and when in the complete opposite direction of where he had been charged to go.
- ✓ His message to the people of Nineveh – to repent and turn to God – is an unqualified success. Which infuriates Jonah such that he wants to die. (Jonah 4:1-3)
- ✓ Many scholars believe this to be an allegory or fictional story due to the style of original writings. Regardless, it is a story of obedience and forgiveness.
- ✓ God's reproach of Jonah in Jonah 4:9-11 is applicable to every one of us at one time or another.

Jonah 2:2-9

"I cried out to the LORD in my great trouble,
and he answered me.
I called to you from the land of the dead,
and LORD, you heard me!
3 You threw me into the ocean depths,
and I sank down to the heart of the sea.
The mighty waters engulfed me;
I was buried beneath your wild and stormy waves.
4 Then I said, 'O LORD, you have driven me from your presence.
Yet I will look once more toward your holy Temple.'

[5] "I sank beneath the waves,
and the waters closed over me.
Seaweed wrapped itself around my head.
[6] I sank down to the very roots of the mountains.
I was imprisoned in the earth,
whose gates lock shut forever.
But you, O LORD my God,
snatched me from the jaws of death!
[7] As my life was slipping away,
I remembered the LORD.
And my earnest prayer went out to you
in your holy Temple.
[8] Those who worship false gods
turn their backs on all God's mercies.
[9] But I will offer sacrifices to you with songs of praise,
and I will fulfill all my vows.
For my salvation comes from the LORD alone."

DANIEL'S PRAYER OF CONFESSION

The Book of Daniel

Facts About Daniel:

- ✓ From the Israelite tribe of Judah, he was taken as a war captive from his country to the foreign country of Babylon.
- ✓ He was of royal nobility; young, handsome, without physical defect, well educated, wise, insightful, and educated in Babylon to speak the language and know the literature. They were to be King of Babylon's servants in the palace.
- ✓ "Daniel" was his Jewish name, but he was renamed and would be known by the Babylonian name "Belteshazzar."
- ✓ Well-cared for, privileged, and obtaining a status few war captives could ever conceive, he was sentenced to death (twice) because of his refusal to relinquish his spiritual standards.

Daniel 9:4-19

"O Lord, you are a great and awesome God! You always fulfill your covenant and keep your promises of unfailing love to those who love you and obey your commands. 5 But we have sinned and done wrong. We have rebelled against you and scorned your commands and regulations. 6 We have refused to listen to your servants the prophets, who spoke on your authority to our kings and princes and ancestors and to all the people of the land.

[7] "Lord, you are in the right; but as you see, our faces
are covered with shame. This is true of all of us,
including the people of Judah and Jerusalem and all
Israel, scattered near and far, wherever you have
driven us because of our disloyalty to you. [8] O LORD,
we and our kings, princes, and ancestors are covered
with shame because we have sinned against you.
[9] But the Lord our God is merciful and forgiving, even
though we have rebelled against him. [10] We have not
obeyed the LORD our God, for we have not followed
the instructions he gave us through his servants the
prophets. [11] All Israel has disobeyed your instruction
and turned away, refusing to listen to your voice.

"So now the solemn curses and judgments written in
the Law of Moses, the servant of God, have been
poured down on us because of our sin. [12] You have
kept your word and done to us and our rulers exactly
as you warned. Never has there been such a disaster
as happened in Jerusalem. [13] Every curse written
against us in the Law of Moses has come true. Yet we
have refused to seek mercy from the LORD our God
by turning from our sins and recognizing his truth.
[14] Therefore, the LORD has brought upon us the disaster
he prepared. The LORD our God was right to do all of
these things, for we did not obey him.

[15] "O Lord our God, you brought lasting honor to your
name by rescuing your people from Egypt in a great
display of power. But we have sinned and are full of
wickedness. [16] In view of all your faithful mercies, Lord,
please turn your furious anger away from your city
Jerusalem, your holy mountain. All the neighboring
nations mock Jerusalem and your people because of
our sins and the sins of our ancestors.

[17] "O our God, hear your servant's prayer! Listen as I
plead. For your own sake, Lord, smile again on your
desolate sanctuary.

18 "O my God, lean down and listen to me. Open your
eyes and see our despair. See how your city—the city
that bears your name—lies in ruins. We make this
plea, not because we deserve help, but because of
your mercy.

19 "O Lord, hear. O Lord, forgive. O Lord, listen and
act! For your own sake, do not delay, O my God, for
your people and your city bear your name."

HABAKKUK'S PRAYER OF ACKNOWLEDGMENT

The Book of Habakkuk

Facts About Habakkuk:

- ✓ Habakkuk was around the same time as Daniel and would be taken away as prisoner to Babylon.
- ✓ Jews, Christians, and Muslims revere him.
- ✓ Considered a "minor" prophet, not because he was "less" than the "major" prophets, but because his actual book is not lengthy.

Habakkuk 3:2-19

2 I have heard all about you, LORD.
I am filled with awe by your amazing works.
In this time of our deep need,
help us again as you did in years gone by.
And in your anger,
remember your mercy.

3 I see God moving across the deserts from Edom,[b]
the Holy One coming from Mount Paran.[c]
His brilliant splendor fills the heavens,
and the earth is filled with his praise.
4 His coming is as brilliant as the sunrise.
Rays of light flash from his hands,
where his awesome power is hidden.
5 Pestilence marches before him;
plague follows close behind.
6 When he stops, the earth shakes.
When he looks, the nations tremble.
He shatters the everlasting mountains
and levels the eternal hills.

He is the Eternal One![d]
7 I see the people of Cushan in distress,
and the nation of Midian trembling in terror.

8 Was it in anger, LORD, that you struck the rivers
and parted the sea?
Were you displeased with them?
No, you were sending your chariots of salvation!
9 You brandished your bow
and your quiver of arrows.
You split open the earth with flowing rivers.
10 The mountains watched and trembled.
Onward swept the raging waters.
The mighty deep cried out,
lifting its hands in submission.
11 The sun and moon stood still in the sky
as your brilliant arrows flew
and your glittering spear flashed.

12 You marched across the land in anger
and trampled the nations in your fury.
13 You went out to rescue your chosen people,
to save your anointed ones.
You crushed the heads of the wicked
and stripped their bones from head to toe.
14 With his own weapons,
you destroyed the chief of those
who rushed out like a whirlwind,
thinking Israel would be easy prey.
15 You trampled the sea with your horses,
and the mighty waters piled high.

16 I trembled inside when I heard this;
my lips quivered with fear.
My legs gave way beneath me,[e]
and I shook in terror.
I will wait quietly for the coming day
when disaster will strike the people who invade us.
17 Even though the fig trees have no blossoms,

and there are no grapes on the vines;
even though the olive crop fails,
and the fields lie empty and barren;
even though the flocks die in the fields,
and the cattle barns are empty,
18 yet I will rejoice in the LORD!
I will be joyful in the God of my salvation!
19 The Sovereign LORD is my strength!
He makes me as surefooted as a deer,[f]
able to tread upon the heights.

JOB'S PRAYER OF CONFESSION

The Book of Job

Facts About Job:

- ✓ The book of Job is most probably the oldest book in the Bible.
- ✓ Job's suffering is identified as "hinam" which is Hebrew for "without reason." (Job 1:9, Job 2:3, Job 9:17) Even by the end of the book God never explains the reasoning for this.
- ✓ The author of Job and the nation of Israel is never mentioned in the book.
- ✓ At a time when the world was thought to be flat, Job's Scripture speaks about a "free floating earth" (Job 26:7) and seems to mention dinosaurs. (Job 40:15-24)

Job 42:1-6

(This is the Message Translation)

"I'm convinced: You can do anything and everything.
Nothing and no one can upset your plans.
You asked, 'Who is this muddying the water,
ignorantly confusing the issue, second-guessing my purposes?'
I admit it. I was the one. I babbled on about things far beyond me,
made small talk about wonders way over my head.
You told me, 'Listen, and let me do the talking.
Let me ask the questions. You give the answers.'
I admit I once lived by rumors of you;
now I have it all firsthand—from my own eyes and

ears!
I'm sorry—forgive me. I'll never do that again, I promise!
I'll never again live on crusts of hearsay, crumbs of rumor."

HANNAH'S PRAYER OF PRAISE

I Samuel 1-2

Facts About Hannah:

- ✓ Hannah was unable to have children at a time when it was thought barrenness was a punishment by God for a sin committed.
- ✓ Even though Hannah's husband loved her, he took a second wife who would give birth to several children.
- ✓ When Hannah first goes to the temple to pray, she is so emotional, the priest thinks she's drunk. (I Samuel 1:14)
- ✓ Hannah promises if the Lord will give her a son, she will give the child back to the Lord. She will keep this promise and, once he is housed in the Temple, she will only be able to see him once a year. (I Samuel 1:24-28)
- ✓ Samuel will go on to become the last of the Israelite judges (who ruled before there were kings) and the first prophet of God.

I Samuel 2:1-10

"My heart rejoices in the LORD!
The LORD has made me strong.[a]
Now I have an answer for my enemies;
I rejoice because you rescued me.
2 No one is holy like the LORD!
There is no one besides you;
there is no Rock like our God.

[3] "Stop acting so proud and haughty!
Don't speak with such arrogance!
For the LORD is a God who knows what you have done;
he will judge your actions.
[4] The bow of the mighty is now broken,
and those who stumbled are now strong.
[5] Those who were well fed are now starving,
and those who were starving are now full.
The childless woman now has seven children,
and the woman with many children wastes away.
[6] The LORD gives both death and life;
he brings some down to the grave[b] but raises others up.
[7] The LORD makes some poor and others rich;
he brings some down and lifts others up.
[8] He lifts the poor from the dust
and the needy from the garbage dump.
He sets them among princes,
placing them in seats of honor.
For all the earth is the LORD's,
and he has set the world in order.

[9] "He will protect his faithful ones,
but the wicked will disappear in darkness.
No one will succeed by strength alone.
[10] Those who fight against the LORD will be shattered.
He thunders against them from heaven;
the LORD judges throughout the earth.
He gives power to his king;
he increases the strength[c] of his anointed one."

PRAYERS FROM OTHER CHRISTIANS

7

RICHARD ROHR'S PRAYER FOR CLARITY

Facts About Richard Rohr:

- ✓ He is an ordained Catholic priest, a Franciscan friar, ecumenical teacher, and prolific author and speaker.
- ✓ He is the founder of the Center for Action and Contemplation.
- ✓ He values "orthopraxis" – the belief that lifestyle and practice are much more important than orthodoxy (the adherence to correct or accepted creeds within a religion). He is critical of Catholic preaching today because he believes this lifestyle and practice is overlooked.

Loving God, we love how you love us.

We love how you free us.

We love what you have given and created to surround us.

Help us to recognize, and to rejoice in, what has been given, even in the midst of what is not given.

Help us not to doubt all that you have given us, even when we feel our very real shortcomings.

We thank you for the promise and sign of your love in the Eternally Risen Christ, pervading all things in the universe, unbound by any of our categories of logic or theology.

We offer you ourselves back in return. We offer you our bodies, our little lives, our racing minds, and our restless hearts into this one wondrous circle of Love that is You.

My life is no longer just about me, but is all about you.[8]

HOWARD THURMAN'S PRAYER TO START THE DAY

Facts About Howard Thurman:

- ✓ He lived from 1899-1981.
- ✓ He was a Baptist minister and prolific author (books, sermons and articles). *Jesus and the Disinherited* was his most famous book but everything he has ever written is fantastic.
- ✓ His ethic of love and non-violence greatly influence Martin Luther King, Jr and other leaders of the Civil Rights Movement.
- ✓ Life Magazine named him as one of the twelve "Greatest Preachers of the 20th Century" in 1953 and Ebony Magazine called him one of the 50 most important figures in African American history.

This day I seek the Lord. I seek to know God that I may understand myself, that I may grasp the true meaning of my own life and have its purpose increasingly defined. I seek His judgment that I may discern an ever clearer meaning between right and wrong courses of conduct. I seek His love that I may be inspired to love more and more what is good and true, and to transcend all barriers which stand between me and my fellows.[9]

HOWARD THURMAN'S PRAYER FOR INSIGHT

Teach me Thy will. Teach me to dig deep enough within me to strike the mainspring of Thy life that flows through me that I may discover Thy Will for my daily living even as for my life. I seek Thy Will in order that I may be whole in my inward parts and that there may be no conflict between the good I see and the good I am…Thus no conflict between my inner and my outer.

Teach me Thy will, O God![10]

HOWARD THURMAN'S PRAYER FOR AN EXEMPLARY LIFE

Kindle Thy light within me, O God, that Thy glow may be spread over all of my life; yea indeed, that Thy glow may be spread over all of my life. More and more, may Thy light give radiance to my flickering candle, fresh vigor to my struggling intent, and renewal to my flagging spirit. Without Thy light within me, I must spend my years fumbling in my darkness.

Kindle Thy light within me, O God![11]

HOWARD THURMAN'S PRAYER OF CONFESSION

The concern which I lay bare before God today is:

My concern for the life of the world in these troubled times.

I confess my own inner confusion as I look out upon the world.

There is food for all – many are hungry.

There are clothes enough for all – many are in rags.

There is room enough for all – many are crowed.

There are none who want war – preparations for conflict abound.

I confess my own share of the ills of the times.

I have shirked my own responsibilities as a citizen.

I have not been wise in casting my ballot.

I have left to others a real interest in making a public opinion worthy of democracy.

I have been concerned about my own little job, my own little security, my own shelter, my own bread.

I have not really cared about jobs for others, security for others, shelter for others, bread for others.

I have not worked for peace; I want peace, but I have voted

And worked for war.

I have silenced my own voice that it may not be heard on the side of any cause, however right, if it meant running risks or damaging my own little reputation.

Let Thy light burn in me that I may, from this moment on, take effective steps within my own powers, to live up to the light and courageously to pay for the king of world, I so deeply desire.[12]

HOWARD THURMAN'S PRAYER FOR THE COMING YEAR

Grant that I may pass through the coming year with a faithful heart.

There will be much to test me and to make weak my strength before the year ends. In my confusion I shall often say the word that is not true and do the thing of which I am ashamed. There will be errors of the mind and great inaccuracies of judgment which shall render me the victim of my own stupidities. In seeking the light, I shall again and again find myself walking in darkness. I shall mistake my light for Thy light and I shall shrink from the responsibility of the choice I make. All of these things, and more, will be true for me because I have not yet learned how to keep my hand in Thy hand.

Nevertheless, grant that I may pass through the coming year with a faithful heart. May I never give the approval of my heart to error, to falseness, to weakness, to vainglory, to sin. Though my days be marked with failures, stumblings, fallings, let my spirit be free so that Thou mayest take it and redeem my moments in all the ways my needs reveal. Give me the quiet assurance of Thy Love and Thy Presence.

Grant that I may pass through the coming year with a faithful heart.[13]

HOWARD THURMAN'S PRAYER FOR VISION

Be Thou my vision this day.

I seek Thy vision not for tomorrow, not for some future day when I am more worthy and more prepared to know and understand. I seek Thy vision this day. Grant to me the flooding of my whole self with the light of Thy countenance that I may know directly when I have missed the way – when I have drifted out of the channel of Thy Purpose.

Be Thou my vision this day![14]

HOWARD THURMAN'S PRAYER FOR CLARITY

Open up to me – light for my darkness.
Open unto me – courage for my fear.
Open unto me – hope for my despair.
Open unto me – peace for my turmoil.
Open unto me – joy for my sorrow.
Open unto me – strength for my weakness.
Open unto me – wisdom for my confusion.
Open unto me – forgiveness for my sins.

Open unto me – tenderness for my toughness.
Open unto me – love for my hates.
Open unto me – thy Self for myself.
Lord, Lord, open unto me![15]

HOWARD THURMAN'S PRAYER FOR COURAGE

The concern I lay bare before God today is my need for courage:

I need courage to be honest-

Honest in my use of words

Honest in accepting responsibility

Honest in dealing with myself

Honest in dealing with my fellows

Honest in my relations with God.

I need courage to face the problems of my own life – the problems of person values:

They are confused

They are often unreal

They are to exacting for comfort

The problems of my job:

Perhaps I am working at cross-purposes with my own desires, ambitions, equipment.

Perhaps I am arrogant instead of taking pride in doing work well.

Perhaps I am doing what I am doing just to prove a point – spending a lifetime to prove a point that is not worth proving after all.

Perhaps I have never found anything that could challenge me, and my life seems wasted.

Here in the quietness I lay bare before God my need for courage, for the strength to be honest, for the guidance to deal effectively with the problems of my own life.

O God, thou wilt not despise![16]

HOWARD THURMAN'S PRAYER FOR BETTERNESS

The concern which I lay bare before God today is my need to be better:

I want to be better than I am in my most ordinary day-by-day contacts:

With my friends-

With my family-

With my casual contacts-

With my business relations-

With my associates in work and play.

I want to be better than I am in the responsibilities that are mine:

I am conscious of my many petty resentments.

I am conscious of increasing hostility toward certain people.

I am conscious of the effort to be pleasing for effect, not because it is a genuine feeling on my part.

I am conscious of a tendence to shift to other shoulders burdens that are clearly my own.

I want to be better in the quality of my religious experience:

I want to develop an honest and clear prayer life.

I want to develop a sensitiveness to the will of God in my own life.

I want to develop a charitableness toward my fellows that is far greater even than my most exaggerated pretensions.

I want to be better than I am.

I lay bare this need and this desire before God in the quietness of this moment.[17]

HOWARD THURMAN'S PRAYER FOR THE WORLD

While we wait in Thy Presence, search our spirits and grant to our minds the guidance and the wisdom that will teach us the way to take, without which there can be no peace and no confidence anywhere.

Teach us how to put at the disposal of Thy Purposes of Peace the fruits of our industry, the products of our minds, the vast wealth of our land and the resources of our spirit.

Grant unto us the courage to follow the illumination of this hour to the end that we shall not lead death to any man's door; but rather may we strengthen the hands of all in high places, and in common tasks seek to build a friendly world, of friendly men, beneath a friendly sky. This is the simple desire of our hearts which we share with Thee in thanksgiving and confidence.[18]

ST. FRANCIS OF ASSISI'S PRAYER FOR PEACE

Facts About St. Francis:

- ✓ He lived from 1181-1226 C.E. and was born into a life of wealth and privilege.
- ✓ Interestingly, he was ordained a deacon but never a priest in the Catholic faith. He is the patron saint of ecology and the environment.
- ✓ He established the Franciscan Order of friars and the women's Order of the Poor Ladies which by the time of his death comprised thousands of friars, sisters, and lay people.
- ✓ Although the below prayer[3] is attributed to St. Francis, many believe that its origins are more recent.

Lord, make me an instrument of your peace.
Where there is hatred, let me sow love,
Where there is injury, pardon
Where there is doubt, faith,
Where there is despair, hope,
Where there is darkness, light,
Where there is sadness, joy.
O Divine Master, grant that I may not so much
seek to be consoled as to console,
not so much to be understood as to understand,
not so much to be loved, as to love;
for it is in giving that we receive,

---

[3] CHECK OUT SARAH MCLAUGHLIN'S SONG OF THIS PRAYER!! https://www.youtube.com/watch?v=agPnMxp5Occ

it is in pardoning that we are pardoned,
it is in dying that we awake to eternal life.[19]

ST. TERESA OF AVILA'S PRAYER ON GETTING OLD

Facts About St. Teresa:

- ✓ She lived from 1515-1582
- ✓ She was a Spanish nun of the Catholic faith, canonized in 1622.
- ✓ She was a prolific reader.
- ✓ In her autobiography she stated, "Just being a woman is enough for my wings to fall off." She was independent and autonomous rejecting authority from anyone but God.

Lord, You know better than I myself
that I am growing older and will someday be old.
Keep me from the fatal habit of thinking
I must say something on every subject and on every occasion.

Release me from craving to
straighten out everybody's affairs.
Make me thoughtful but not moody;
helpful but not bossy.

With my vast store of wisdom,
it seems a pity not to use it all;
but You know, Lord,
that I want a few friends at the end.
Keep my mind free from the recital of endless details;
give me wings to get to the point.

Seal my lips on my aches and pains;
they are increasing, and love of rehearsing them
is becoming sweeter as the years go by.

I dare not ask for improved memory,
but for a growing humility and a lessening cock-
sureness
when my memory seems to clash with the memories
of others.
Teach me the glorious lesson that occasionally I may
be mistaken.

Keep me reasonably sweet, for a sour old person
is one of the crowning works of the devil.
Give me the ability to see good things in unexpected
places
and talents in unexpected people;
and give, O Lord, the grace to tell them so.

Amen.

ST. TERESA'S PRAYER WHEN YOU ARE FRIGHTENED

Let nothing disturb you,
let nothing frighten you,
all things will pass away.
God never changes;
patience obtains all things,
whoever has God lacks nothing.
God alone suffices. Amen.[20]

FRANCINE GIORELLO'S PRAYER OF HOPE & BELIEF

<u>Facts About Francine:</u>

- ✓ I am privileged to be able to call her one of my dear eternal sisters-in-Christ.
- ✓ She states that the below prayer "is a prayer/mantra that I repeat often, especially when I am not feeling as stated…it's a prayer of hope and belief that I am and/or will be happy, healthy and healed.

I am happy.

I am healthy.

I am healed.

I am confident in the Lord.

I eat right.

I exercise.

I drink my water.

I am forever grateful.

CHRISTINA ROSSETTI'S PRAYER FOR LIFE

Facts About Christina Rossetti:

- ✓ She lived from 1830-1894, in England.
- ✓ She was a poet, as was her father.
- ✓ She published her first poem as a teen and would make a choice to never marry.
- ✓ She died of breast cancer.

What can I give Him,

    Poor as I am?

If I were shepherd

    I would bring a lamb.

If I were a Wise Man

    I would do my part.

Yet what can I give Him?

    Give my heart.[21]

(This is only a portion of the poem In The Bleak Midwinter.)

MARTIN LUTHER'S PRAYER FOR TRANSFORMATION

Facts About Martin Luther King:

- ✓ He lived from 1483-1546
- ✓ His father wanted him to be a lawyer.
- ✓ Although a priest of the Church of Rome (Catholic), he would receive credit for starting the Reformation which resulted in the split that became the Catholic and Protestant religions. (Although issues had been percolating for a while.) He is the "father" of the Lutheran religion.
- ✓ His "95 Theses" (indictments against the Church of Rome) would spread quickly through Europe, in part because of the development of the printing press.
- ✓ He would marry a nun name Katharina von Bora, as a continual flouting of the Church of Rome's edicts.

Behold, Lord, An empty vessel that needs to be filled.
My Lord, fill it. I am weak in faith; Strengthen thou me.
I am cold in love; Warm me and make me fervent
That my love may go out to my neighbour.
I do not have a strong and firm faith; At times I doubt and am unable to trust thee altogether.
O Lord, help me. Strengthen my faith and trust in thee.
In thee I have sealed the treasures of all I have.
I am poor; Thou art rich and didst come to be merciful to the poor.
I am a sinner; Thou art upright.
With me there is an abundance of sin; In thee is the

fullness of righteousness.
Therefore, I will remain with thee of who I can receive but to whom I may not give. Amen.[22]

MARYLYNN OUDHEUSDEN'S BEDTIME PRAYER (S)

Facts About Marylynn Oudheusden:

- ✓ She's my Mom!
- ✓ For my entire life, she has been the Woman of Faith that I have determined to emulate. I'm still working on getting to her level!
- ✓ Her family nickname, THE MACHINE, is a nod at her spiritual and personal strength in the face of a lifetime of coping with situations and unavoidable realities that would have crushed the typical human.
- ✓ Her favorite food on the entire planet is Turkey Hill Chocolate Peanut Butter ice cream. She is a woman of excellent taste!
- ✓ This is the bedtime prayer she taught me as a child. The other version (… "if I should die before I wake, I pray the Lord my soul to take") I never heard until I was grown. She made this one up because she felt it was more loving and peaceful.
- ✓ The second prayer is one I found that she had cut out and saved by her bedside.

Now I lay me down to sleep,
I pray the Lord my soul to keep.
And as I go through each new day,
I pray the Lord to guide my way. Amen.[23]

I lie down this night with God,
And God will lie down with me;
I lie down this night with Christ,
And Christ will lie down with me;
I lie down this night with the Spirit,
And the Spirit will lie down with me;
God and Christ and the Spirit
Be lying down with me.

ST. AUGUSTINE OF HIPPO'S PRAYER FOR DIRECTION

Facts About St. Augustine:

- ✓ He lived from 354 to 430 C.E.
- ✓ He was born in Algeria to a Christian mother and a pagan father.
- ✓ At one point in his life, he fathered a child out of wedlock, abandoned the Christian faith, and stole.
- ✓ In 386 he converted to Christianity and in 391 he was ordained as a priest where he would eventually found a monastery.
- ✓ "Hippo" was the location of his diocese and actually means "horse."

Lead us, O God, from the sight of the lovely things of the world

To the thought of thee their Creator;

And grant that delighting in the beautiful things of thy creation,

we may delight in thee, the first author of beauty and the Sovereign Lord of all thy works, blessed for evermore.[24]

MOTHER TERESA'S PRAYER ON HOW TO LIVE

Facts About Mother Teresa:

- ✓ She lived from 1910 to 1997.
- ✓ She was canonized by the Catholic faith in 2016.
- ✓ Originally from Albania, she took her vows as a nun in 1931, and in 1946 determined to serve the poor in India for the rest of her life.
- ✓ In 1948 she set aside her nun's habit and adopted the simple style of sari and sandals, choosing to live in a rented hovel in the slums.
- ✓ In her original school for the poor, she taught the children to read and write by writing in the dirt with sticks.
- ✓ Her Missionaries of Charity was a hospice for the poor, a refuge for sufferers of leprosy, and a home for orphans and homeless youth.

People are often unreasonable, irrational, and self-centered. Forgive them anyway.

If you are kind, people may accuse you of selfish, ulterior motives. Be kind anyway.

If you are successful, you will win some unfaithful friends and some genuine enemies. Succeed anyway.

If you are honest and sincere people may deceive you. Be honest and sincere anyway.

What you spend years creating, others could destroy overnight. Create anyway.

If you find serenity and happiness, some may be jealous. Be happy anyway.

The good you do today, will often be forgotten. Do good anyway.

Give the best you have, and it will never be enough. Give your best anyway.

In the final analysis, it is between you and God. It was never between you and them anyway.[25]

ELIZABETH ELLIOT'S PRAYER FOR PATIENCE

Facts About Elizabeth Elliot:

- ✓ She was born in Belgium, into a missionary family.
- ✓ She lived from 1926-2015 and was a Christian author and speaker.
- ✓ Her first husband, Jim Elliot, was killed on a missionary journey in Ecuador. She later spent two years as a missionary with that same tribe that killed her husband.

Loving Lord and heavenly Father, I offer up today all that I am, all that I have, all that I do, and all that I suffer, to be Yours today and Yours forever.

Give me grace, Lord, to do all that I know of Your holy will.

Purify my heart, sanctify my thinking, correct my desires.

Teach me, in all of today's work and trouble and joy, to respond with honest praise, simple trust, and instant obedience, that my life may be in truth a living sacrifice, by the power of Your Holy Spirit and in the name of Your Son Jesus Christ, my Master and my all.

Amen.[26]

PRAYER OF ST. IGNATIUS OF LOYOLA FOR SURRENDER

Facts About St. Ignatius

- ✓ He lived from 1491-1556.
- ✓ He was a Spanish Catholic priest and theologian and founder of the religious order The Society of Jesus, aka The Jesuits.
- ✓ Prior to becoming a priest, he was a soldier and embraced a lifestyle absolutely contrary to what he would later devote his life to.
- ✓ His conversion came about while convalescing from surgery and reading a religious work which inspired him to devote himself to God and follow the example of Francis of Assisi.

Take, Lord, and receive all my liberty,
my memory, my understanding,
and my entire will,
All I have and call my own.

You have given all to me.
To you, Lord, I return it.

Everything is yours; do with it what you will.
Give me only your love and your grace,
that is enough for me.[27]

ST. PATRICK'S PRAYER FOR UNITY WITH CHRIST

Facts About St. Patrick:

- ✓ He was actually born in England, taken as a slave to Ireland and after his freedom would go back to Ireland as a priest.
- ✓ He lived from 387-461 C.E.
- ✓ He never officially attained sainthood by the Catholic Church.
- ✓ He never really did that snake thing… (there were no snakes in Ireland).

I arise today through a mighty strength, the invocation of the Trinity,
Through a belief in the Threeness, Through confession of the Oneness
Of the Creator of creation.

I arise today through the strength of Christ's birth and His baptism,
Through the strength of His crucifixion and His burial,
Through the strength of His resurrection and His ascension,
Through the strength of His descent for the judgment of doom.

I arise today through the strength of the love of cherubim,
In obedience of angels, in service of archangels,
In the hope of resurrection to meet with reward,
In the prayers of patriarchs, in preachings of the apostles,

In faiths of confessors, in innocence of virgins,
In deeds of righteous men.

I arise today through the strength of Heaven
the rays of the sun, the radiance of the moon,
the splendor of fire, the speed of lightening,
the swiftness of the wind, the depth of the sea,
the stability of the earth, the firmness of rock.

I arise today through the power of God:
God's might to comfort me, God's wisdom to guide me,
God's eye to look before me, God's ear to hear me,
God's word to speak for me, God's hand to lead me,
God's way to lie before me, God's shield to protect me,
God's Heavenly Host to save me from the snares of the devil,
from temptations to sin, from all who wish me ill,
from near and afar, alone and with others.

May Christ shield me today against poison and fire,
against drowning and wounding, so that I may fulfill my mission
and bear fruit in abundance.
Christ behind and before me,
Christ behind and above me,
Christ with me and in me,
Christ around and about me,
Christ on my right and on my left,
Christ when I lie down at night,
Christ when I rise in the morning,
Christ in the heart of every man who thinks of me,
Christ in the mouth of everyone that speaks of me,
Christ in every eye that sees me,
Christ in every ear that hears me.

I arise today through a mighty strength, the invocation of the Trinity,

Through belief in the threeness, through confession of the oneness,
Of the Creator of Creation.[28]

PRAYER ON SPECIFIC TOPICS

29

PRAYERS OF ENCOURAGEMENT

Facts About Encouragement:

- ✓ "Encouragement" is the action of giving someone support, confidence, or hope.
- ✓ It can be an act of persuasion or stimulation to get someone to do or to continue to do something.
- ✓ Joshua 1:9 says, "Be strong and courageous. Do not be frightened, and do not be dismayed, for the Lord your God is with you wherever you go."

May the road rise up to meet you.

May the wind be always at your back.

May the sun shine warm upon your face.

May the rains fall soft upon your fields,

And until we meet again,

May God hold you

In the palm of His hand. (Traditional Irish Blessing)

May the Lord bless you and keep you.

May the Lord make his face to shine upon you, and be gracious to you.

May the Lord lift up his countenance upon you and give you peace. (Numbers 6:24-26)

Whoever you are and wherever you go in God's wide world know this:

Christ goes with you

Before you to prepare your path;

Behind you to encourage you;

Beside you to befriend you;

Above you to watch over you;

Beneath you [in troubled times] to carry you;

And most importantly

Within you to give you His abiding and abundant peace, now and forevermore. Amen

(This is a variation of St. Patrick's Prayer.)

PRAYERS ON TRANSFORMATION

<u>Facts About Transformation:</u>

- ✓ "Transformation" usually means "a complete or major change in someone or something's appearance, form." BUT, "Transformation" in the Bible has nothing to do with our outward behavior or self-improvement.
- ✓ "Transformation," according to what the Bible means, is more closely compared to a caterpillar's transformation into a butterfly – it is a total change from one type of human being to another.

Our Father, Thou knowest our nature and readest our innermost thoughts, and nothing can be hidden from Thee; help us, then, to unburden ourselves of every disguise we wear before the world, and find strength in being what we are, Thy humble and grateful children. Enable us to put off sham and pretense. Be patient with any of us who still prefer vain shows and empty pride to the freedom and security of Thy Truth.

Enable us to carry out from this place peace and strength that here we gain. Because we have talked with Thee here, may we be able to work more patiently for Thy Kingdom, bringing light upon the problems that perplex the world, dispelling the night of doubt and fear with They sheltering love.

Amen. (Howard Thurman)

Lord, teach me how You want me to live. Let me be steadfast and trustworthy, and let my integrity be a sign that You have made me new, in Your image. Amen. (Dan Dick)

O Lord, help me to know You, and through knowing You, help me to be like You. Make me a faithful, loving follower, and be with me to guide me this day, and every day to come. Amen. (Dan Dick[4])

I want to practice Your presence. Engage with my heart day and night and teach me how to be more sensitive to Your leading. I want it to be obvious to everyone around me that I have been in Your presence by the fruit that manifests in my life. (Jennifer LeClaire)

Father, maker of light,

It's dark outside in the world.

Son, light unmade and eternal,

Illumine m steps lest I stumble.

Spirit, inner flame of Pentecost,

Feed your fiery tongues of inner light and

Cleanse me for praise and service.

Amen. (Calvin Miller)

O Lord God, destroy and root out whatever the Adversary plants in me, that with my sins destroyed you may sow understanding and good work in my

---

[4] Copywrite attributes do not necessarily identify the writer, but the author of the book in which the prayer was found.

mouth and heart; so that in act and in truth I may serve only you and know how to fulfill the commandments of Christ and to see yourself. Give me memory, give me love, give me chastity, give me faith, give me all things which you know belong to the profit of my soul, O Lord, work good in me, and provide me with what you know that I need. Amen. (Calvin Miller)

Dear Christ,

Who can see into every heart and read every mind,

Take hold of my thoughts,

Bring my thoughts back to me,

And clasp me to yourself. (Calvin Miller)

I am bending my knee

In the eye of the Father who created me,

In the eye of the Son who purchased me,

In the eye of the Spirit who cleansed me,

In friendship and affection. (Esther DeWaal)

PRAYERS ON PATIENCE

Facts About Patience:

- ✓ The word "patience" comes from the Old French *pacience* and the Latin word *patientia* and refers to "the quality of suffering or enduring; submission" also indulgence, leniency; humility; submissiveness; literally "quality of suffering."[30]
- ✓ The word "patient" is connected to patience; and can be either a noun (a suffering, injured, or sick person under medical treatment) or an adjective (capable of enduring misfortune, suffering, etc., without complaint.)[31]
- ✓ The phrase, "Patience is a virtue" is not in the Bible! Its origin is hard to conclusively identify; maybe Cato the Elder in the 3rd or 4th century or The Canterbury Tales written in the 14th century.

Dear Lord,

Help me to relax about insignificant details, beginning tomorrow at 7:41:23 a.m. EST.

Help me to consider people's feelings, even if most of them are hypersensitive.

Help me to take responsibility for the consequences of my actions,
even though they're usually not my fault.

Help me to not try to run everything – but, if you need some help, please feel free to ask me.

Help me to be more laid back, and help me to do it exactly right.

Help me to take things more seriously, especially laughter, parties, and dancing.

Give me patience, and I mean right now!

Help me not be a perfectionist. (Did I spell that correctly?)

Help me to finish everything I start.

Help me to keep my mind on one thing … oh, look, a bird … at a time.

Help me to do only what I can, and trust you for the rest. And would you mind putting that in writing?

Keep me open to others' ideas, misguided though they may be.

Help me follow established procedures. Hey, wait … this is wrong …

Help me slow down andnotrushthroughwhatido.

Thank you, Lord.

Amen (Anonymous)

Holy Spirit, help me to recognize Father's timing so that I don't rush ahead of His will. Help me not grow weary in doing good so that I can reap in due season. Help me to hold on to the great and precious promises He has given me. (Jennifer LeClaire)

PRAYERS OF PRAISE

Facts About Praise:

- ✓ Another word for praise is "worship".
- ✓ God wants us to worship. (See the next point!)
- ✓ Worship/Praise is one of the most important ways of loving God.
- ✓ Read Psalm 100:1. Praise and worship aren't always formal and isn't only done on Sunday during church service!
- ✓ John 4:23-24 says we are to worship God in spirit and in truth.
- ✓ Worship/Praise also involves surrendering to God – giving God everything.

Oh God of the elements,
O God of the mysteries,
O God of the fountains,
O King of Kings!
Thunder is the laughter of power.
Lightning is God say, "Now can you see my majesty?"
Lord, let my limitations
Borrow from your greatness,
I am content to trust You in the storms. (Calvin Miller)

Thanks be to Thee, Jesu Christ,
For the many gifts Thou hast bestowed on me,

Each day and night, each sea and land,
Each weather fair, each calm, each wild.
I am giving Thee worship with my whole life,
I am giving Thee assent with my whole power,
I am giving Thee praise with my whole tongue,
I am giving Thee honour with my whole
utterance. (Esther DeWaal)

Glory be to the Father,
And to the Son,
And to the Holy Spirit.
As it was in the beginning,
It is now,
And ever shall be,
World without end. Amen (Gloria Patri)

PRAYERS ON TRUST

Facts About Trusting:

- ✓ Trust in God, first, foremost, and only, is the key to success in life. Relying only on ourselves is a recipe for disaster. Proverbs 3:5-6
- ✓ Trust eradicates fear, anxiety, and worry. Philippians 4:6-7
- ✓ God's already got life planned out for each one of us. Jeremiah 29:11-14

Those who trust in the Lord will never be disappointed. I choose this day to trust in You for the grace I need to rise up and handle everything You expect me to do – and for the courage to say no to those things You have not called me to do. (Jennifer LeClaire)

You're right: I can't figure it all out. I need You! Open my eyes so I can see what You are trying to show me. Give me a spirit of wisdom and revelation in the knowledge of Christ. Lead me into all truth. I am asking and listening. (Jennifer LeClaire)

PRAYERS ON PEACE

Facts About Peace:

- ✓ Jesus spoke specifically about peace. John 14:27, 16:33
- ✓ Peace goes hand in hand with trust. Isaiah 26:3
- ✓ Jesus lauded those who are peacemakers. Matthew 5:9
- ✓ Jesus' peace in believers' hearts is something to be thankful for. Colossians 3:15

God shield the house, the fire, the kine,

Every one who dwells herein to-night.

Shield myself and my beloved group,

Preserve us from violence and from harm;

Preserve us from foes this night.

In this place, and in every place where in they dwell to-night,

On this night and on every night,

This night and every night. (Calvin Miller)

I am lying down tonight with the Holy Spirit,

And the Holy Spirit this night will lie down with me,

I will lie down this night with the Three of my love,

And the Three of my love will lie down with me. (Calvin Miller)

Our Father, I would sleep tonight in the knowledge that I will wake on some shore and whether I wake in the land of angels or earthlings, I am grateful you will be near me at the waking and I will offer praise to whatever dawn I see to whatever world gives me the new light and a warm sun. Amen. (Calvin Miller)

PRAYERS ON RIGHT LIVING

Facts About Godly Living:

- ✓ Believers are specifically told to be not of this world. Jesus describes it as being "salt and light." Matthew 5:13
- ✓ Believers are to be distinctly different/unique from nonbelievers. Romans 12:2
- ✓ The evidence of the Spirit within us is: love, joy, peace, patience, kindness, goodness, and faithfulness. Galatians 5:22
- ✓ The life Jesus Christ lived while on earth is the epitome of how a human being is to be. John 14:6

Bless to me, O God,

My soul and my body; Bless to me, O God,

My belief and my condition; Bless to me, O God,

My heart and my speech.

And bless to me, O God,

The handling of my hand; Strength and busyness of morning,

Habit and temper of modesty,

Force and wisdom of thought,

And Thine own path, O God of virtues,

Till I go to sleep this night; Thine own path, O God of virtues,

Till I go to sleep this night. (Esther DeWaal)

Let not my words be a trap for me, but let me act in a way pleasing to You. There is nothing that needs to be said, only love needs to be shown. (Dan Dick)

Lord, make my behavior good and acceptable. Help me to see the errors in my thinking and acting. Bring me to an understanding. (Dan Dick)

Lord, guide the steps of my feet. Help me to remember that the eyes of other people are on me. When I dishonor You, I dishonor the entire faith. Forgive me. Amen. (Dan Dick)

Holy Spirit, Your fruit is faithfulness. You are faithful, even when I am not faithful. Help me to draw from You everything I need to walk worthy of my calling in Christ and run my race in such a way that I will be counted faithful in the end. (Jennifer LeClaire)

PRAYERS ON FORGIVENESS

Facts About Forgiveness:

- ✓ There is nothing that we can do that God will not forgive. I John 1:9
- ✓ Believers are called to this same level of forgiveness in our relationships with others. How we forgive is how God will forgive us. Matthew 6:14-15
- ✓ Forgiveness is a reflection of love. Ephesians 4:31-32

Thank You for revealing forgiveness as a weapon of warfare. Help me to use this mighty weapon to pull down the strongholds in my soul that are contrary to Your love. I will not hold ought against anyone. I choose to forgive today and every day. (Jennifer LeClaire)

PRAYERS ON CONFIDENCE

<u>Facts About Confidence:</u>

- ✓ A believer, anchored in God, cannot fail. Isaiah 41:10
- ✓ A believer, anchored in God, can do all things. Philippians 4:13
- ✓ A believer, anchored in God, has confident hope. Romans 15:13
- ✓ All things, work together for good, for those who love God and are called according to God's purpose. Romans 8:28

Lord, there is no seedling in the thicket that does not call you its maker. And I, too, come knowing that whatever the quality of my life, is, it is thou, O God, who stamped your purpose on my soul. So I must praise you lest the silent stones grow tongues and do what I would not. Amen. (Calvin Miller)

Our Father,

Encompass me with joy, for weeping gathers all is gloom against me.

Encompass me with love, for the world's a hating place at times.

Encompass me with summer, for there is too much ice in secularity.

Encompass me with goodness, for the days overwhelm the soul with negativity.

Encompass me with foreverness, for I am too temporary to have any kind of future without you.

Amen (Calvin Miller)

Father, help me not to fear the road that leads to your most perfect pleasure. May the road rise up to meet me, then may you walk the road with me. I mind no journey kept by two, if one of them is you. Amen (Calvin Miller)

Jesus, encircle me with your strength that I might follow your instructions in this day. I lay my trembling soul on the breast of God, knowing I am born into a family in which the Spirit, who sired me, has raised a hedge of steel around my fragile being. God has drawn a wondrous circle around me and set me down in the middle of it. And you, my brother Christ, are the encicler, making the circle so powerful that demons stop at its circumference. Even hell draws back within those smaller boundaries drawn long ago by a Roman cross. Lord, help me feel the power of the encircling today that I might obey you. Amen. (Calvin Miller)

Be thou a bright flame before me,

Be though a guiding star above me,

Be though a smooth path below me,

And be a kindly shepherd behind me,

To-day, to-night, and forever. (Calvin Miller)

PRAYERS ON THANKS

Facts About Thankfulness:

- ✓ Believers are to be thankful in all circumstances, trusting that the Spirit is with us guiding us and protecting us. I Thessalonians 5:18
- ✓ Every good and perfect gift is from God. James 1:17
- ✓ We are unconditionally, eternally loved. Psalm 107:1, 118:1

God, I do not presume to pretend that I understand everything that You do. Your will is far beyond my comprehension. Thank You for loving me enough to make me a part of Your great creation. Walk with me and be with me this day, and all the days to come. Amen. (Dan Dick)

Each thing I have received, from Thee it came.

Each thing for which I hope, from Thy love it will come.

Each thing I enjoy, it is of Thy bounty.

Each think I ask, comes of Thy blessing. (Calvin Miller)

Thanks be to you, our Lord Jesus Christ,

For all the benefits which you have given us,

For all the pains and insults which you have borne for us.

Most merciful Redeemer, Friend, and Brother,

May we know you more clearly,

Love you more dearly,

And follow you more nearly,

Day by day. Amen

(The prayer of St. Richard, Bishop of Chichester, from the 13th century.)

PRAYERS FROM OTHER FAITHS[32]

A JEWISH PRAYER OF HOW TO LIVE YOUR LIFE

Facts About The Jewish Faith:

- ✓ Genesis 14:13 is the first time the term "Hebrew" is used and it is used in reference to Abraham and the root letters mean to "cross over" or "pass through." This is perhaps in reference to the fact that Abraham traveled from his birthplace to a distant land at God's command.
- ✓ The English term "Jew" comes from the Hebrew term "Yehudi, meaning "from the Kingdom of Judah."
- ✓ There are three main branches within Judaism: Reform (most "liberal"), Conservative and Orthodox Jews (most "conservative").

You shall love Adonai your God

With all your heart, with all your soul,

And with all your might.

And these words

Which I command you today

Shall be in your heart.

You shall teach them diligently to your children

And you shall speak of them

When you are sitting at home

And when you go on a journey.

When you lie down

And when you rise up.

You shall bind them as a sign on your hand

And they shall be jewels between your eyes.

You shall inscribe them on the doorposts

Of your home and on your gates. (Shira Shoenberg)

Hear, O Israel: The Lord is our God, the Lord alone. Deuteronomy 6:4

A HINDU PRAYER OF FORGIVENESS

Facts About The Rig Veda

- ✓ There are 4 Vedas, ancient scriptures of Hinduism, and the Rig Veda is the earliest, largest and most important of them.
- ✓ The Rig Veda is a collection of 1028 hymns in praise of the gods, which is chanted in various rituals.
- ✓ Origination is probably in the region of present-day Pakistan, between 1500 and 1200 BCE.
- ✓ "God the Supreme" existed before creation, is the creator, protector and ruler of this world, and among numerous other qualities is omnipotent, omniscient, transcendent, and incomparable.

If we have ever been mean to one who loves us,
Ever wronged a fried or playmate,
The child next door or a stranger,
O Lord, take away our sin.
If we have ever cheated at our games,
Not meaning to or on purpose,
Take away our sin, O Lord,
And let us be your own beloved children.

A BUDDHIST PRAYER OF FORGIVENESS

Facts About Buddhism:

- ✓ Siddhattha Gotama (c.563 BCE-c.483 BCE) was the founder of Buddhism.
- ✓ Buddha, ("Awakened One") is someone who is completely free from all faults and mental obstructions and sees things as they really are. There are many people who have become Buddhas in the past (and will in the future).
- ✓ Some do not recognize Buddhism as an organized religion, but rather, a "way of life" or a "spiritual tradition.
- ✓ Buddha's most important teachings are known as The Four Noble Truths: the truth of suffering, the truth of the cause of suffering, the truth of the end of suffering, the truth of the path that frees us from suffering.
- ✓ "Dharma" means "protection" and by practicing Buddha's teachings we protect ourself from suffering and problems.

When someone is wronged, he must put aside all resentment and say,

"My mind shall not be disturbed;

No angry word shall escape my lips;

I will remain kind and friendly,

With loving thoughts

And no secret spite."

AN AMERICAN INDIAN PRAYER FOR HUMANITY

Facts About the Native American People:

- ✓ Much of Native American religious beliefs are without sacred texts, fixed doctrines or moral codes and are found in societies without wealth, writing, or systems of politics or justice or any of the usual indicators of civilization making the wealth of traditions difficult to retain and inspire.
- ✓ The history of this people is also marked by loss after centuries of political, economic, and religious domination from others.
- ✓ For many native communities, religion is understood as the relationship between living humans and other persons or things, however they are conceived. Besides the so-called "natural world" there are "mythic beings" understood to inhabit and affect either this world or some other world contiguous to it.
- ✓ Religious practices are highly localized, impossible to number, and linguistically diverse.

O Great Spirit,
Whose voice I hear in the winds,
And whose breath gives life to all the world,
Hear me! I am small and weak, I need your
Strength and wisdom.

Let Me Walk In Beauty, and make my eyes ever behold the red and purple sunset.

Make My Hands respect the things you have made and my ears sharp to hear your voice.

Make Me Wise so that I may understand the things you have taught my people.

Let Me Learn the Lessons you have hidden in every leaf and rock.

I Seek Strength, not to be greater than my brother, but to fight my greatest enemy – myself.

Make Me Always Ready to come to you with clean hands and straight eyes.

So When Life Fades, as the fading sunset, my spirit may come to you without shame.

AN AMERICAN INDIAN PRAYER ON GRATITUDE

Our religion is all about thanking the Creator.

That's 'what we do when we pray.

We don't ask Him for things.

We thank Him.

We thank Him for the world and every animal and

plant in it. We thank Him for everything that exists.

We don't take it for granted that a tree's just there. We thank the Creator for that tree.

If we don't thank Him maybe the Creator will take

that tree away. That's what the ceremonies are all about—that's why

they are important—even for the White Man

We pray for the harmony of the whole world.

The Creator wants to be thanked… (Leon Shenandoah, (Esther DeWaal))

A MUSLIM PRAYER OF THANKS AND GRATITUDE

Facts About Islam:

- ✓ The word "Islam" means "submission to the will of God."
- ✓ Those who follow Islam are called Muslims.
- ✓ Muslims are monotheistic and worship one God who they recognize as Allah.
- ✓ Islam teaches that Allah's word was revealed through the prophet Muhammad (via the angel Gabriel), and also respect some Jewish and Christian prophets such as Abraham, Moses, Noah, and Jesus.
- ✓ The Quran is the major holy text of Islam.

Bismillah Al-Rahman Al-Raheem
In the name of God the most Merciful the Beneficent.

Oh Nourisher and Provider of all things.
We offer our thanks and gratitude for this food, and for those who prepared it.

In a world where so many are hungry, may we eat this food with humble hearts.

We offer our thanks and gratitude for each member of our community and the opportunity that we all have to come together to do good.

Dear God, may you bless our efforts and help us sit present with one another, mindful of our purpose.

Bismillahi'wa' ala Barakatillah
In the name of God and with the blessings of God, Let us begin.

- Tamara Mahmoud, Xavier Graduate '17 offered at Xavier Board of Trustees and student dinner, Feb. 16, 2017[33]

ABOUT THE AUTHOR

Susan McGeown is a wife, mother, daughter, sister, friend, aunt, uncle (don't ask), teacher, author … but, most importantly, a "woman after God's own heart." Always working on a new book, she writes historical novels (including Rosamund's Bower, 2008 RCRW's Golden Rose winner in the category of 'Novel with Romantic Elements'), contemporary fiction novels, and nonfiction Bible studies.

She's been a teacher, a conference leader, a public speaker, a children's minister, a deacon, an elder, a vacation Bible school coordinator, a preschool director, a Bible study leader and, most recently, a seminary student. Writing, researching, and speaking is still just about the best way she can imagine spending her time.

Living in Bridgewater, New Jersey, with her husband of over thirty years, each of Sue's stories champions those emotions nearest and dearest to her: faith, joy, hope and love.

Philippians 1:20-21: I earnestly expect and hope that I will in no way be ashamed but will have sufficient courage so that now, as always, Christ will be exalted in my life. For me, to live is Christ and to die is gain.

BIBLIOGRAPHY

Bible Gateway New Revised Standard Version. (1989). (Division of Christian Education of the National Council of the Churches of Christ in the USA) Retrieved 1 16, 2020, from https://www.biblegateway.com

Bible Hub. (2004-2016). Retrieved from https://biblehub.com

Bibles, C. (2001). *Open Bible.* Retrieved from Topical Index: https://www.openbible.info/topics/

Common English Bible. (2013). Nashville: Common English Bible.

De Waal, E. (1997). *The Celtic Way of Prayer.* New York: The Crown Publishing Group.

Dick, D. (1986). *Wisdom From The Bible.* Uhrichsville, OH: Barbor Publishing.

Harrelson, W. J. (Ed.). (2003). *New Revised Standard Version with the Apocrypha (New Interpreter's Study Bible).* Nashville, TN: Abingdon Press.

Jseuitresource.org. (2022, May 22). Retrieved from Muslim Prayers: https://www.xavier.edu/jesuitresource/online-resources/prayer-index/muslim-prayers

LeClaire, J. (2015). *Mornings With The Holy Spirit.* Lake Mary, FL: Charisma.

Miller, C. (2008). *Celtic Devotions.* Downers Grove: IVP Books.

New Century Version Holy Bible. (2003). Fort Worth : Thomas Nelson Bibles.

Peterson, E. H. (2002). *The Message.* 2012: Nav Press.

Rohr, R. (2013). *Yes, And...* Cincinnati: Franciscan Media.

Schoenberg, S. (2022, May 20). *Jewish Virtual Library*. Retrieved from jewish Prayers: The Shema: https://www.jewishvirtuallibrary.org/the-shema

The Online Etymology Dictionary. (2022, May 20). Retrieved from https://www.etymonline.com/word/patience

Thurman, H. (1981). *Meditations of the Heart.* Boston: Beacon Press.

Thurman, H. (2006). *Essential Writings.* Maryknoll, NY: Orbis Books.

Tutu, D. (2011). *God Is Not A Christian & Other Provocations.* New York: Harper One.

FOOTNOTES

---

[1] (Thurman, Essential Writings, 2006), *The Inward Sea,* pg. 136-137
[2] The Comforter, Michael Dudash Art
[3] All Scripture quoted is from the New Revised Standard Version of the Bible unless otherwise noted. (Bible Gateway New Revised Standard Version, 1989)
[4] (Common English Bible, 2013)
[5] (Common English Bible, 2013)
[6] (Peterson, 2002)
[7] Praying Girl, Roberto Ferruzzi
[8] (Rohr, 2013), pg. 261
[9] (Thurman, Meditations of the Heart, 1981), pg. 205
[10] (Thurman, Meditations of the Heart, 1981), pg. 214
[11] (Thurman, Meditations of the Heart, 1981), pg. 160
[12] (Thurman, Meditations of the Heart, 1981), pp. 196-197
[13] (Thurman, Meditations of the Heart, 1981), pg. 96
[14] (Thurman, Meditations of the Heart, 1981), pg. 191 – this is a *partial* quote.
[15] (Thurman, Meditations of the Heart, 1981), pg. 188-189
[16] (Thurman, Meditations of the Heart, 1981), pg. 194-195
[17] (Thurman, Meditations of the Heart, 1981), pg. 193-194
[18] (Thurman, Meditations of the Heart, 1981), pg. 188, this is a *partial* quote.
[19] https://www.loyolapress.com/catholic-resources/prayer/traditional-catholic-prayers/saints-prayers/peace-prayer-of-saint-francis/
[20] https://www.ewtn.com/catholicism/devotions/prayer-of-saint-teresa-of-avila-364
[21] This is only a portion of the poem *In the Bleak Midwinter* by Christina Rossetti. Read the full poem here: https://www.poetryfoundation.org/poems/53216/in-the-bleak-midwinter
[22] https://acollectionofprayers.com/2016/06/20/the-empty-vessel/
[23] Marylynn Oudheusden – my wonderful Mom!!
[24] https://www.gantshillurc.co.uk/ministers-blog/prayers-of-saint-augustine-of-hippo
[25] https://www.prayerfoundation.org/mother_teresa_do_it_anyway.htm
[26] https://www.commonwaychurch.com/lent2020-9-2/
[27] https://www.providence.org/about/providence-archives/history-online/mother-joseph-of-the-sacred-heart/her-last-days/prayer-of-st-ignatius
[28]

https://www.journeywithjesus.net/PoemsAndPrayers/Saint_Patrick_Prayer.shtml
[29] Golden Rule, Norman Rockwell
[30] The Online Etymology Dictionary
[31] The Online Etymology Dictionary
[32] Woman In Prayer, Myfa Therzson
[33] (Jseuitresource.org, 2022)

Made in the USA
Middletown, DE
21 November 2023

43103423R00066